WILD WHEELS

DODGE VIPERS

By Bob Power

Gareth Stevens
Publishing

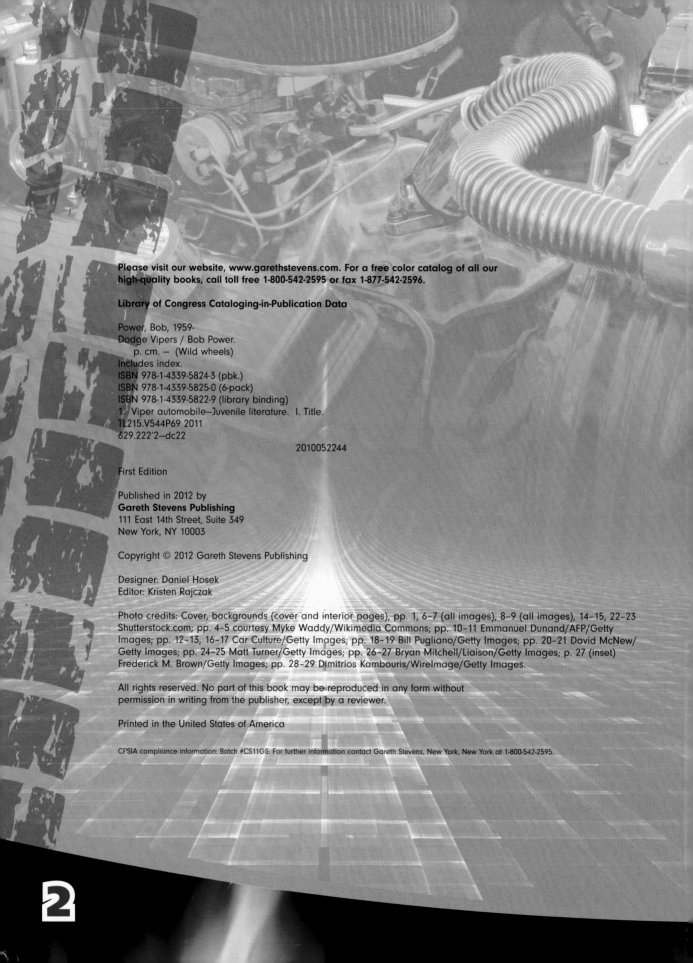

Please visit our website, www.garethstevens.com. For a free color catalog of all our high-quality books, call toll free 1-800-542-2595 or fax 1-877-542-2596.

Library of Congress Cataloging-in-Publication Data

Power, Bob, 1959-
Dodge Vipers / Bob Power.
   p. cm. — (Wild wheels)
Includes index.
ISBN 978-1-4339-5824-3 (pbk.)
ISBN 978-1-4339-5825-0 (6-pack)
ISBN 978-1-4339-5822-9 (library binding)
1. Viper automobile—Juvenile literature. I. Title.
TL215.V544P69 2011
629.222'2—dc22

                              2010052244

First Edition

Published in 2012 by
Gareth Stevens Publishing
111 East 14th Street, Suite 349
New York, NY 10003

Copyright © 2012 Gareth Stevens Publishing

Designer: Daniel Hosek
Editor: Kristen Rajczak

Photo credits: Cover, backgrounds (cover and interior pages), pp. 1, 6–7 (all images), 8–9 (all images), 14–15, 22–23 Shutterstock.com; pp. 4–5 courtesy Myke Waddy/Wikimedia Commons; pp. 10–11 Emmanuel Dunand/AFP/Getty Images; pp. 12–13, 16–17 Car Culture/Getty Images; pp. 18–19 Bill Pugliano/Getty Images; pp. 20–21 David McNew/Getty Images; pp. 24–25 Matt Turner/Getty Images; pp. 26–27 Bryan Mitchell/Liaison/Getty Images; p. 27 (inset) Frederick M. Brown/Getty Images; pp. 28–29 Dimitrios Kambouris/WireImage/Getty Images.

Printed in the United States of America

CPSIA compliance information: Batch #CS11GS: For further information contact Gareth Stevens, New York, New York at 1-800-542-2595.

CONTENTS

Words in the glossary appear in **bold** type the first time they are used in the text.

The Viper

Have you ever seen a Dodge Viper? The Viper is a small, stylish car, but it's also very powerful. In fact, it's one of the fastest cars on the road today. The Viper introduced in 2010 can go from 0 to 60 miles (97 km) per hour in less than 4 seconds!

Dodge Viper symbol

The Viper gets its name from a type of snake. These snakes are known for their powerful bite. Ever since they were introduced in 1992, Dodge Vipers have been known for their powerful engines. They were the first cars to use a V-10 engine!

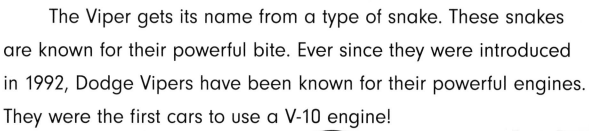

INSIDE THE MACHINE

The Viper's V-10 engine was based on the V-10 truck engine. However, after it was made stronger and lighter, the Viper's V-10 hardly resembled the truck engine. The changes enabled the engine to go faster.

The Dodge Viper is meant to remind drivers of the great American sports cars of the 1960s.

A V-10 Engine

A V-10 engine has 10 **cylinders**. The cylinders are arranged in two **banks** of five cylinders each. When gasoline is burned, a **piston** inside each cylinder moves up and down. This makes the energy that powers the car. The pistons turn a part called a crankshaft, which carries power to the wheels.

The Viper's V-10 was built for speed!

Dodge Viper engine

The Viper's V-10 engine is unusually large for a car. Many cars run on a V-6 or V-8 engine. These engines have fewer cylinders and provide a lot less power than a V-10. There are also engines with more cylinders than the V-10, such as the V-12.

INSIDE THE MACHINE

Engines with all the cylinders in a row are called in-line engines. In a "V" engine, the two banks of cylinders are angled in a V shape. V engines are smaller than in-line engines. This allows more room for other features.

Sleek Coupes and Roadsters

Sports cars like the Viper are built for speed, not for carrying around lots of people. In fact, the Viper only has room for two people. This makes it lighter and faster than ordinary cars. Vipers can be either **roadsters** or **coupes**. The coupes have a metal top, while the roadsters don't. Both have only two doors.

All Vipers have a sleek look. They're low cars with big wheels. This helps them grip the ground at high speeds. The wheels are made of strong but light **aluminum**. The car's curved body shape is **aerodynamic**.

This Viper is a roadster with its top in place.

INSIDE THE MACHINE

Have you ever ridden in a convertible, or a car with no top? It can be a great way to spend a sunny day! Dodge Viper roadsters come with a soft top that can be attached to keep drivers warm and dry on cold or rainy days.

Shelby and the Cobra

The Dodge Viper was partly modeled on a sports car from the 1960s called the Cobra. The Cobra had been **designed** by a famous sports car creator named Carroll Shelby. Shelby had started out as a very successful car racer during the 1950s before he took up design.

Cobras, such as this 1965 coupe, can sell for millions of dollars!

The first Cobra was made in 1962. It was a two-door roadster. The Cobra's body was made by the British company AC Cars, and its engine was made by the American carmaker Ford Motor Company. In 1964, a coupe model was introduced. Cobra coupes and roadsters won several important car races during the 1960s.

INSIDE THE MACHINE

Shelby has said that the name "Cobra" came to him in a dream in 1962. Like a viper, a cobra is a kind of snake. The Cobra roadster was the fastest road car of its time.

A Great Concept

In 1982, Shelby started working with Dodge. In 1987, he started thinking about the car that would become the Viper. Over the next 2 years, Shelby worked with the team that produced the Viper concept car. A concept car is a car built to show a new design and features that may one day be used in cars sold to the public.

Dodge showed off the Viper concept car in January 1989 at the North American International Auto Show in Detroit, Michigan. The car was a big hit! It was much faster, sleeker, and more powerful than any other car Dodge was making at that time.

Chrysler, the company that owned Dodge, needed new cars to improve its image. During the 1970s and much of the 1980s, Chrysler had made safe family cars. The company wanted to make something exciting for a sporty crowd. The Viper was just that.

This 1992 Viper was part of Chrysler's new image in the 1990s.

The First Vipers

In January 1992, Dodge started selling the Viper RT/10. These first Vipers were roadsters. They looked a lot like the concept car from 1989. Like the concept car, RT/10s had no door handles on the outside of the car and no side windows.

This 2002 Viper roadster doesn't look much different from the first RT/10s.

However, there were a few key differences. The RT/10's rearview mirrors were larger than the concept car's, which made it easier for drivers to see behind the car. The concept car still had the heavy iron V-10 engine that had been designed for trucks. The Viper RT/10 used a V-10 engine that was made of lighter aluminum.

INSIDE THE MACHINE

The engine in the Viper RT/10 was designed by the Italian carmaker Lamborghini. At that time, Chrysler owned Lamborghini. The aluminum engine increased the Viper's **horsepower** from 300 to 400.

The GTS

In 1996, Dodge introduced the Viper GTS coupe. The new Viper had a double-bubble roof. This means that it had a bump over each seat. There were other changes, too. The GTS's engine and body both weighed much less than they had in the first Vipers. This means the GTS could **accelerate** even more quickly! Also, the **exhaust pipe** was moved to the rear of the car. Earlier Vipers had side exhaust pipes.

The GTS also had air bags to make the car safer. In 1997, air bags were also added to the RT/10.

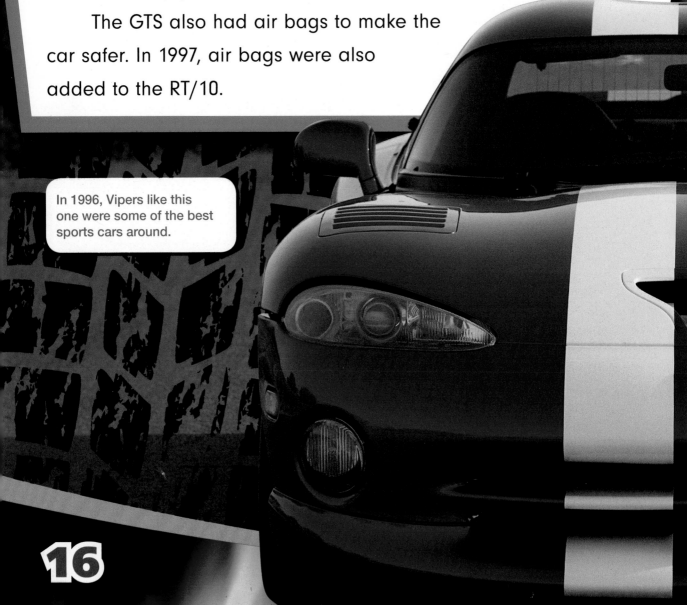

In 1996, Vipers like this one were some of the best sports cars around.

Dodge knew that lightweight cars were some of the speediest around. The Viper GTS needed to be lighter in order to gain more speed. An all-aluminum **suspension system** helped the GTS lose some of its weight. Redesigning the engine and cooling system removed another 80 pounds (36 kg).

The SRT 10

Dodge made more changes to the 2003 Viper. It had a new name, too. It was called the Viper SRT 10. The new Viper had a more modern, less rounded look. It also had a new 500-horsepower engine. The new engine wasn't only more powerful than the old one—it was larger.

The first SRT 10s were roadsters. The Viper SRT 10 coupe made its first appearance in 2006. The coupe also had the new engine and other improvements featured in the roadster.

The SRT 10 coupe was introduced at the 2005 North American International Auto Show.

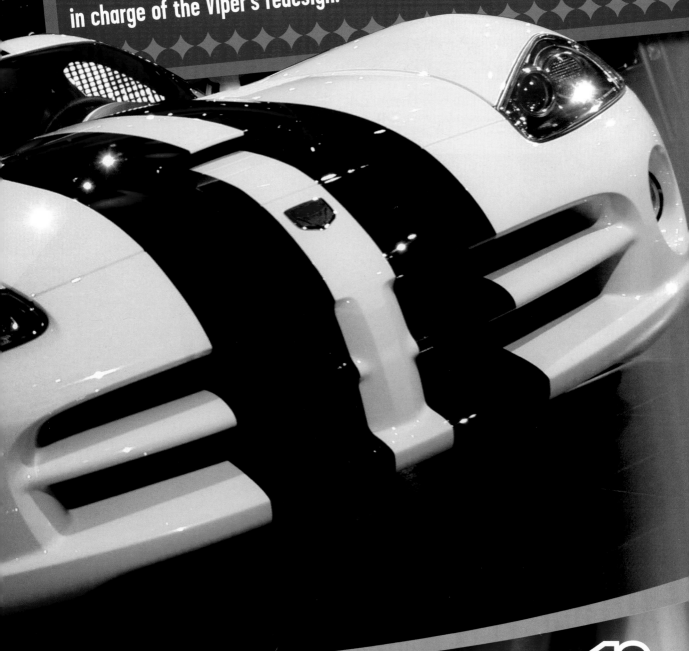

INSIDE THE MACHINE

The "SRT" part of the SRT 10's name came from the initials of Chrysler's Street and Racing Technology division. This was the part of the company in charge of the Viper's redesign.

Improving the SRT 10

In 2008, the Viper got an even more powerful engine. This new engine was also bigger than the one in the first SRT 10 and produced a mind-blowing 600 horsepower! It could zoom from 0 to 60 miles (97 km) per hour in less than 4 seconds.

The new SRT 10 model competed with the newest Corvette ZR1, also introduced in 2008.

The car had a newly designed plastic hood. It had larger vents and scoops. These are openings in the hood that let in air. The air helps keep the engine cool and increases the car's horsepower. The Viper's body panels were also made of plastic and other light materials. This helped keep the car from getting too heavy.

INSIDE THE MACHINE

Vipers are very expensive cars. In 2010, their cost started at more than $90,000. Part of the cost included a "gas guzzler" tax because of the car's poor **fuel efficiency**.

The Viper ACR

Along with the basic models, there have been several specially produced Vipers. One of the most popular has been the Viper ACR. It was introduced in 1999. ACR stands for American Club Racer. These cars were built for owners who mainly wanted to race the

wing

The Viper ACR's rear wing was larger and longer than usual car wings.

cars on racetracks. They had added features such as special air filters, springs, and powerful **shock absorbers**. The special features pushed the first Viper ACRs' horsepower to 460. The cars could still be driven on normal roads, though.

Dodge kept making ACRs in most of the following years. In 2010, the ACR-X was introduced. It's a special ACR made only for the racetrack.

INSIDE THE MACHINE

The 2010 Viper SRT 10 ACR's top speed was more than 200 miles (322 km) per hour! The car had a "rear wing" that made it more aerodynamic, and its engine could produce 600 horsepower.

On the Track

The Viper has been linked to racing from the very beginning. In 1991, one of the first Vipers ever made was used as the pace car at the Indianapolis 500. A pace car leads racers around the track to warm up their engines but doesn't join the race.

Later Vipers actually competed on the racetrack. Some of them were very successful. The Viper GTS-R won in its class in a French race called the 24 Hours of Le Mans in 1998, 1999, and 2000.

This Viper GTS-R raced in the Asia Pacific Le Mans Series in 2000.

INSIDE THE MACHINE

Today, many of the Vipers used in racing are Viper Competition Coupes. They can go from 0 to 60 miles (97 km) per hour in 3.8 seconds! These coupes aren't allowed to drive on the street.

A Star Car

Thanks to its speed and power, the Viper has won a place in the hearts of many drivers. The Viper has also been featured in several movies, such as the 2006 TV movie *Drake and Josh Go Hollywood*. In 2005, a movie all about the car came out. It was called *Dodge Viper: A Legend in Its Own Lifetime*.

The Viper was even the star of a TV show! The show *Viper* aired during the 1990s. It was about a Viper that turned into a crime-fighting machine called the "Defender." A red RT/10 roadster and a blue GTS coupe starred in the show at different times.

This Viper RT/10 is just like the one used in the TV show *Viper*!

INSIDE THE MACHINE

The Viper that was featured in *Drake and Josh Go Hollywood* was red 2003 Dodge Viper SRT 10. In the movie, the main characters s the car from professional skateboarder Tony Hawk.

Drake Bell

Josh Peck

The Viper's Future

In 2010, Dodge announced that a redesigned version of the Viper would be introduced for 2013. No one knew what it would look like, but Viper fans were relieved. Before the announcement, there had been talk that Vipers might no longer be made.

The future now looks bright for the Viper. That's good news for car lovers everywhere. The Viper's pairing of a simple but stylish design with a hugely powerful engine has delighted fans for many years. With luck, it will continue to win fans for years to come.

In 2004, more than 100 Viper owners gathered in South Salem, New York, to show off their cars.

INSIDE THE MACHINE

Dodge Viper lovers can join the Viper Club of America. They meet up at car shows and other events to talk about Vipers and check out each other's cars.

Glossary

accelerate: to increase in speed

aerodynamic: having a shape that improves airflow around a car to increase its speed

aluminum: a type of lightweight metal

bank: a group of things that are lined up

coupe: a two-door car with one section for the seat and another for storage space

cylinder: one of the tube-like spaces for pistons in an engine

design: to create the pattern or shape of something. Also the shape of an object.

exhaust pipe: a tube through which the smoky air made by burning gas or other fuels escapes from the engine

fuel efficiency: the quality of being able to operate using little fuel, or without waste

horsepower: a measurement of an engine's power

piston: a piece in an engine that slides up and down inside the cylinder as it makes power for the engine

roadster: an open car with just two side doors

shock absorbers: parts that make a car's ride less bumpy

suspension system: springs and other devices on a car that reduce the shaking and bumping caused by uneven roads

For More Information

Books

Anderson, Jameson. *Dodge Viper*. Mankato, MN: Capstone Press, 2008.

Maurer, Tracy. *Viper*. Vero Beach, FL: Rourke Publishing, 2007.

Woods, Bob. *Hottest Sports Cars*. Berkeley Heights, NJ: Enslow Publishers, 2008.

Websites

Dodge Vipers at Allpar
www.allpar.com/cars/viper/
Learn how the Dodge Viper came to be one of the best-loved American sports cars.

How Car Engines Work
www.howstuffworks.com/engine.htm
See diagrams and read a description about the inner workings of a car engine.

Viper Club of America
www.viperclub.org
Find out more about the official club for Dodge Viper owners.

Index